D'ap. J. Alus au sarcophage au muséum du pape

4.e Cinq Dessins

THE STORY OF NIOBE

◇——◇

ADAPTATIONS FROM
OVID'S METAMORPHOSES
BY
BRETT RUTHERFORD,
PHILLIS WHEATLEY,
& SAMUEL CROXALL

EDITED AND ANNOTATED
BY
BRETT RUTHERFORD

YOGH &
THORN
BOOKS

PITTSBURGH, PENNSYLVANIA

THE STORY OF NIOBE

Phillis Wheatley, age 20, in a portrait engraved in London in 1773 for the first edition of her *Poems on Various Subjects*.

INTRODUCTION

I HAVE LIVED WITH the story of Niobe since around 2005, when I undertook the study of Phillis Wheatley's poetry in a graduate class with Prof. Marty Rojas at University of Rhode Island. As a poet and long-time admirer of the Greek and Roman classics, I immediately identified with the one poem by the slave poet of Boston that was least approachable to most modern readers: her re-writing of a singularly gruesome episode in Ovid's *Metamorphoses*. This story of queenly hubris that encompasses blasphemy against old gods, fourteen murders, a royal suicide, and a petrifaction, runs against the grain of most of her other poems, which are occasional or religious, the productions expected by her Christian sponsors who preferred the Biblical to the Classical.

When questioned, Wheatley said *she* preferred the classics. She studied Latin, and most likely used the 1717 English edition of *The Metamorphoses* edited by Sir Thomas Garth, to help her fashion her own adaptation from the Latin. She re-ordered some of the elements into a mini-epic and added details not in Ovid, but instead based on her viewing of an engraved copy of an influential painting, Richard Wilson's *Niobe*. The details on how Wheatley adapted Ovid's Latin, and the ekphrastic use of images from the painting, are explored in my essay, "Niobe's Tears: The Classical Poetry of Phillis Wheatley," later in this volume. An early version of this article was presented at a graduate student conference at University of Rhode Island in 2006, and a later version became part of my Master's portfolio in 2007. Further work was done when I added new material about Wheatley's poems addressed to two English sailors. This version was published in *Sensations Magazine* in 2009, as part of that journal's ongoing research series on American poetry since the 16th Century.

Omitted from all these versions was a surprise discovery I made just as I was completing the graduate portfolio: that Paul Revere's famous engraving of The Boston Massacre copies key details from the Wilson Niobe painting, and that the verse included on the print personified Boston as a weeping shawled woman, who might be a Niobe-like figure. The 1770 Revere print has no proven connection to Wheatley, of course, but it does demonstrate how the classical discourse of which *Metamorphoses* is a part, was sufficiently powerful and universal to be used as a visual cue, a rhetoric

<9>

employing a vocabulary of images. In this discourse, if one said, "Weeping, like ...?" the respondent would very likely reply, "Niobe."

It was easy for poets of the 17th and 18th centuries to repeat the Niobe story as an example of hubris punished, especially royal hubris, but the cruelty and carnage wreaked by Latona and her offspring do not permit the translator or reader to fold it into Christian thought as a fable. The Abbé Banier, in his 1732 explication of all of Ovid's "fables," instead proposes that the story has its basis in many episodes of plague in the ancient world, and that sudden death of men was oft described as an act of Apollo, and that of women as an act of Artemis.

This, however, does not describe the lurid appeal of the individual deaths, meted out in Homeric detail for the sons of Niobe (but in rather delicate restraint for the death of the daughters, whom Ovid does not even name.) I read the poem instead as a fable about the cruelty of arbitrary power, which appealed to Wheatley's sense of injustice as a slave, herself kidnapped as a child from her African mother.

Additionally, I read the poem as one of those clashes between Titans and Olympians from a world in which an old Chthonic religion had given way to the calmer world of Zeus and Hera and the nuclear family of key gods. Figures like Niobe and Latona, who are, or claim heritage from, Titans, act as wild cards and agents of chaos. Their cruelty is second-nature.

Just recently, I came upon the 2009 version of my paper, and the sketches for the ancillary Paul Revere notes. The latter is now a separate article in this book, with illustrations to explain the connection between Revere's print and the Wilson *Niobe*.

Looking over my hand-written notes, I discovered another, which said, "To understand what Wheatley had to do in order to translate *Niobe*, make your *own* version from the Latin." This I have done now, just days ago, in my own manner, and I found that I was spontaneously adding new lines and thoughts as I went, filing in gaps, embellishing, all while largely following the Latin in the order it was written. My poem is no less "true" to Ovid than Croxall's, although I have taken far more liberties than Wheatley. There were gaps in Ovid, a lack of scene painting, even a lack of transition between scenes. There are dead bodies, and suddenly they are on biers. The place of Latona's worship is not described, so I took the liberty to portray her temple as a more primitive structure with a rough-hewn sculpted image of Latona. And having just completed some adaptations from Anglo Saxon and Old Danish poetry, I was struck by the absence of the crows, ravens. wild dogs and wolves that would be expected to gather the moment the ground was littered with engored dead bodies. So I went where Ovid would not, and speculated that the people of Thebes would have fled the scene in horror and abandoned the dead bodies to scavengers.

<10>

I did some annotations on proper names and history in my translation, but I do not repeat those footnotes in the Wheatley or Croxall, so the reader interested only in Wheatley would do well to at least scan my footnotes. In both Wheatley and Croxall I have retained their period spelling except for a few words that seemed too awkward or odd not to modernize. Since my own version broke neatly into scenes, I added divisions and numbers to Wheatly and Croxall where possible to achieve the same end, although both of those poets, like Ovid, composed their poems as a continuous narrative. Wheatley's poem sub-divides readily into six-line stanzas, an ease to reading.

In the "Bookseller's Preface" to a 1732 multi-lingual Ovid, the editor notes the liberties that all translators have taken:

> in a few Places ... the Translators have either thought *Ovid* absolutely not worth Translating at all, and so have left out Passages: Or else his Thoughts too low to require a laboured Translation: Or Lastly, where more Images occurred to the Translator, than had done to the Poet himself, and thus lengthened out the Description: For the Genius of a Poet, and That of his Translators being seldom of a Size, or equally animated in the same Descriptions, will produce all These and sometimes much greater Diversities.

The story of Niobe and her children, collectively called "The Niobids," was a major inspiration for artists from antiquity to the present day, who took up the challenge of god, goddess, queen and fourteen victims in sculpture, funerary monuments, paintings, vases, tapestries and other media. I wish I could view the one at the Palazzo d'Arco in Mantua described thus: "The Mantuan Zodiac Room has a frieze of the utmost decorative intensity, showing little episodes from Ovid against a black background, like Pompeian murals or cameos, separated by monsters of fearsome invention" (Godwin, 67).

A few of these representations decorate this book. The paintings post-date Wheatley's poem, so we should bear in mind that she knew only Wilson's modest painting, which added a few dimly-seen figures from the myth into a storm-tossed landscape.

Poetry serves many ends, and in this troubled year, a poem concerning itself with the boasts of a narcissist ruler, sudden death from on high, civil despair, and cruel gods, seems to be a suitable offering.

Brett Rutherford
August 1, 2020
Pittsburgh, PA

<11>

THE STORY OF NIOBE

by Brett Rutherford (2020)
Adapted from Book VI of Ovid's Metamorphoses

1. OF THE PRIDE OF NIOBE

A woman turned to a spider![1] Whoever heard of such a thing?
All the towns in Lydia trembled at the horror of it. It spreads
through Phrygia, the shattered pride of Arachne, daring to spin
and embroider in contest with Pallas Athena. Self-hanged
in spite, she is doomed to six-leggedness, to sit hungry always
at the heart of a dread weaving all know to be a place of poison.
You would think her friend and playmate Niobe, might weep
to recall how they ran the fields of Maeonia together,
and drank the bees' nectar in the shadow of Mount Sipylus.

Yet the girl learned nothing from the sad example of how
the wise, concerning gods, should speak little and praise much.
Niobe had what some call pride of place,
      beside an artful spouse,
queen in her realm, high born and married to Thebes, but these
were motes of arrogance beside her pride of motherhood.
None need call out she was the most blessed of mothers,
since she so frequently uttered it herself. Fourteen times
fruited was her matronly belly, once even twinned!

---

[1] *A woman turned to a spider.* This stanza is the connecting passage from the
preceding episode in Book VI, the story of Arachne.

<13>

a rock that floated hither and yon for centuries.
The land did not want her. The sea denied her.
The starry universe spat at the sound of her name.
And what did Latona do? She bore two children. *Two.*
I have done seven times that, and might do more.
Happy am I, and blessed, and happy shall I be.

"Why ask anything of all-but-forgotten gods
when you are safe with me, too great
and too well-descended to fear bad luck?
If drought comes, the stores are full. It passes.
If sickness comes, we heal the sick. Bright day
erases the drear fog of the night of the dead.

"Suppose some part of my tribe of children
might be taken from me? Take two, take four.
I still have five times as many as she! Latona,
as such things go, is practically *childless!*

"Go back to your looms, and to the market,
go back to your homes and gardens," Niobe demands.
"Cast off the laurels as you pass the door.
I will hear no more of Latona."

The women obey, and yet they mumble the name
of the slighted Titaness instead of that
of the proud and angry Queen of Thebes.
Manto, alone, falls to her knees and weeps.

<16>

At Cynthus,[7] in her austere dwelling
high on the peak of a prodigious cliff,
Latona waits the waft of incense, and the bees'
murmur of far-off Theban prayers, too soon
ended and not enough to satisfy. Then up
to her ears by Echo carried comes Niobe's speech.
Each laurel thrown to the temple floor, each
stooped retreat without the proper obeisance
is a slap in Latona's face. How fair a face?
One need but look at Apollo and Artemis
formed in her guise in high relief. From her
the beauty that stuns to silence, from force
unknown beyond the universe, the arts divine
inspired by the sun-bright siblings. "You two!"
her mother summons them, and fast they fly
as quick as thought and waves of energy.

They reach for her embrace; she shivers off
all contact in the ice of her anger. "You two,
my pride and joy, you know that I bow
to no one but Hera, knowing my place
that others many know and honor theirs.
Hear how my divinity has been tarnished,
my temple insulted, my prayers snuffed out.

"This Niobe, spawn of Tantalus, who crept
like a dog to sup on the gods' apples, daughter
of a thief of table scraps, you she insults, too,
preferring her own grown sons and daughters
to the elder gods she should at least give nod to
and pass by in silence if she cannot praise.

"No Apollo, no Artemis she honors: she calls me
childless, in bloat of pride just like a sow
who loses count of her many piglets and swells
to name and number them lords of the sty.
Just like her father, she is swollen with hubris."

---

[7] *Cynthus.* The mountain on Delos where Latona gave birth to Apollo.

<17>

More would Latona have said, but Phoebus
Apollo with lifted hand stops her. "Enough!
Each moment spent in hearing more, delays
the moment of Latona's punishment. Let's go!"
So saying, he seizes his sister's hand, and off
they fly. Sooner than a man could harness
two horses to a chariot, they came to Thebes,
concealed in cloud above the tower of Cadmus.

<18>

3. OF THE DEATH OF THE SEVEN SONS

It was a field of Mars where they but played at war,
the exercising grounds of Latona's athletic sons.
Crowds gathered daily to watch their chariots,
the shows of archery, the wrestling and races.
Truly, they seemed like gods at play. The earth
was flat and dry where horses' hoofs and wheels
packed down the dust and clay. Only a few trees
and shrubs dotted the open plain, the city walls
in plain view behind it. King Amphion seldom came,
but many idled and watched as princes rode
horseback in Tryrian purple, turning and racing
with their tight gold-coated bridles. Ismenus,
first-born, his mother's favorite son, rode wide
along the curved track, as if to race against
any or all of his brothers. Hard he pulled the bit,
the foam'd mouth of the young stallion resisted.
He squinted once at the single cloud, the only one
marring the sky's perfection of azure, then sat
upright and cried as the first arrow struck him,
red on purple and straight through the heart.

What can one say of the arrows of Apollo,
and those of his sister, no less in power?
Unleashed, they always strike their target.
Not even a zephyr would dare to deflect
the path from archer's eye to the target.
Only another god, invisible, could nudge
the victim to safety in the eye-blink between
the harp twang of string and the heart-pierce
of flesh-rending bronze. And so, "Ah, me!"
was all Ismenus said, as he sank sideways downward
over the shoulder of his astonished horse.

<19>

His brother, Sipylus made out the fatal sound
of the arrow-laden quiver within the cloud,
and giving rein, fled for the city walls,
just as a captain turns sail away and flees
from a sudden storm. How many hoof-beats
and how fast would take him to safety? Too slow,
too late, as the unavoidable arrow took him.
The arrow shaft sang as it sliced his neck.
Only a gurgling noise escaped him as the point
thrust out through his Adam's apple. Forward
he pitched and his own horse trampled him.
His warm blood gushed in the dry ground's gullies.

Elsewhere upon the playing field, two brothers fond
who loved nothing more than trading triumphs
and sweet defeats as well-oiled wrestlers
were at a sweaty match, each goaded on by friends
and adherents. "Go Phaedmus!" some called.
"Tantalus! Be like your grandsire! Invent some trick
to tumble your brother under foot! On, Tantalus!"
The brothers strained together, breast to breast,
their breathing as heavy as lovers', their eyes intent
for one another's stumbling weakness. There was not
the track of an ant between them when both inhaled,
swelling their huge frames, as just one arrow,
one perfect, impossible arrow, sped from the bow
of Artemis intent to outshine her brother. One arrow
impaled them both. They groaned in unison, eyes locked
upon one another in disbelief. Naked they fell.
Their last breath was a mutual exhalation.

Helpless Alphenor watched them die, and from the crowd
rushed forth, He beat his breast and crying, "My brothers!
My brothers!" he marked himself for ready death. He leaned
to lift the stone-dead bodies of Phaedmus and Tantalus,
and just as if he had carried them to their grave
the spot he stood on became his own death. One arrow
from Apollo plowed through his midriff at perfect center,
a bull's eye hit that sent him groaning to slow
and painful death-agonies. Someone ran bravely

<21>

She lifted bruised arms, all bronzed with gore
to the never-moving storm-cloud, then turned
her face toward where Latona's temple stood,
hurling her imprecation so loud the very walls
of Thebes were shocked, and trembled.

"Feast now upon my grief, Latona, cruel
beyond the imagination of Tartarus,
feast and glut your heart with my sorrow.
It is endless — it will feed you forever!
Seven sons now I must burn and bury,
sevenfold my suffering. Exult, victorious
only in hatred. Your name shall be cursed
as the by-word for cruelty. Feast then,
and fill your empty heart with my sorrow.

"But, ha! your victory is not a victory.
My misery is greater still than your contentment
off in that place where no one knows your name.
Who will come to your temple now? Doors boarded
up, its walls leaning every which way, in years
to come it will be a ruin, a chicken-coop.
"After so many deaths, I triumph still!
Seven sons gone, I still have seven daughters!"

<24>

The day advanced, and dusk drew near. Cut trees
and timbers carried forth from the city took shape
into seven hastily-made biers, and the seven sisters,
robed in black, their faces smeared with weeping,
gathered around the scene of horror. All heard
the sky-shaking throb of the bowstring on high,
and one,[8] while drawing out the arrow from inside
her brother's raven-torn innards, toppled dead
before any saw that a missile had stricken her.
Some thought she merely fainted, but others saw
the pulsing flow of blood beneath her.

Another as she stood next her grieving mother
was cut down just as suddenly. Dim light
and enfeebl'd sight made some assume
the daughters were passing out with grief.

Latona's daughter died before her, lips clenched,
without a word of reproach or a farewell cry.
One tried to flee, hoping her robes of black
would vanish into twilight. So *she* fell, too,
and her sister, hard upon her, tumbled down
and both, in a heap, were arrowed, expiring.
One hid, but from the overarching cloud
there was no shelter; *she* fell. One stood
defiant, until the angry shaft toppled her.

---

[8] *One*. As a mark of Ovid's, or Rome's, misogyny, none of Niobe's daughters are
given names in the text. The deaths of the sons are accorded Homeric details, but
the daughters are anonymous and interchangeable. Apollodorus names them
Astycrateia, Ogygia, Phthia, Naera or Cleodoxa, Pelopia, Astyoche, and Ethodaia,
All the children of Niobe are referred to as The Niobids. A more generous take
on Ovid here is that he is in haste to get on with his narrative, and that it might
be in bad taste to describe a young woman's disembowelment.

<25>

Now six had suffered wounds, and bleeding,
died. Niobe raced to her last daughter's side.
The girl crouched, and Niobe tried to drape
her blood-stained robe to cover her.
Niobe screamed to the heavens again. "Latona!
Or you who come to slaughter in Latona's name!
Just leave me one, the smallest, she is nothing
to you, my last vestige on earth. The littlest
one I beg you to spare me! Just one!" Yet even
as she prayed for the mercy of the implacable,
another shaft fell, sure aimed, rending her robe
and killing the hidden, crouching girl beneath it.

<26>

6. Of the Petrifaction of Niobe

Now sits Niobe, childless truly, amid the gore
of fourteen slaughtered children, the sons on biers,
the daughters scattered in bloody pools
as wolf and dog, crow and raven, red-eyed,
begin their death caw, the taste for flesh
that attends every battlefield. None dare to move,
except to melt away to their darkened homes,
where, hearths extinguished, the Thebans sat
sleepless and transfixed with terror.

Niobe sees one bier she had not noticed:
the self-slain Amphion from whom no sons
or daughters more could issue, fate sealed
upon Niobe's curse forever. Silence was all
amid the creeping night, the ominous wingbeats
of carrion seekers. What horror at dawn
when the night's feasting would be revealed!

Sun rises on the unpeopled field of Mars.
The birds are at their business. A wary wolf
circles the motionless Niobe.

Her hair, a mass of blood clots, does not move.
There is no breeze to stir it. Her face grows pale
as though her own blood had gone to ground.
Her eyes are fixed on nothing. She does not stir.
Aside from her, the picture is void of human life. Eyes
frozen, tongue locked in roof of mouth, teeth
clenched on final horror, she weeps. She weeps.
She wills her neck to bend — it disobeys;
she orders her arms to move, but they will not.

Her legs and feet are frozen. Slowly her heart,
the proud heart and all her innards, petrify.
She is nothing but a rockpile in woman's form,
but still she weeps. Tears of their own accord
flow out and down the semblance of face.

<27>

During the night that followed, some gods
took pity and lifted the weeping Niobe on high
dropping her back to a hillside in Phrygia,
where she weeps still, and forever,
a perpetual spring in a wall of limestone.

Who learns not from the lessons of punished Pride
must pay the toll of sorrow and extinction!

<29>

NIOBE, IN DISTRESS FOR HER CHILDREN SLAIN BY APOLLO

by Phillis Wheatley (1773)

1

Apollo's wrath to man the dreadful spring
Of ills innum'rous, tuneful goddess, sing!
Thou who did'st first th' ideal pencil give,
And taught'st the painter in his works to live,
Inspire with glowing energy of thought,
What Wilson painted, and what Ovid wrote.

Muse! lend thy aid, nor let me sue in vain,
Tho' last and meanest of the rhyming train!
O guide my pen in lofty strains to show
The Phrygian queen, all beautiful in woe.
'Twas where Maeonia spreads her wide domain
Niobe dwelt, and held her potent reign:

See in her hand the regal sceptre shine,
The wealthy heir of Tantalus divine,
He most distinguish'd by Dodonean Jove,
To approach the tables of the gods above:
Her grandsire Atlas, who with mighty pains
Th' ethereal axis on his neck sustains:

<31>

Her other grandsire on the throne on high
Rolls the loud-pealing thunder thro' the sky.
Her spouse, Amphion, who from Jove too springs,
Divinely taught to sweep the sounding strings.
Seven sprightly sons the royal bed adorn,
Seven daughters beauteous as the op'ning morn,

As when Aurora fills the ravish'd sight,
And decks the orient realms with rosy light
From their bright eyes the living splendors play,
Nor can beholders bear the flashing ray.
Wherever, Niobe, thou turn'st thine eyes,
New beauties kindle, and new joys arise!

But thou had'st far the happier mother prov'd,
If this fair offspring had been less belov'd:
What if their charms exceed Aurora's teint.
No words could tell them, and no pencil paint,
Thy love too vehement hastens to destroy
Each blooming maid, and each celestial boy.

Now Manto comes, endu'd with mighty skill,
The past to explore, the future to reveal.
Thro' Thebes' wide streets Tiresia's daughter came,
Divine Latona's mandate to proclaim:
The Theban maids to hear the orders ran,
When thus Maeonia's prophetess began:

"Go, Thebans! great Latona's will obey,
And pious tribute at her altars pay:
With rights divine, the goddess be implor'd,
Nor be her sacred offspring unador'd."
Thus Manto spoke. The Theban maids obey,
And pious tribute to the goddess pay.

<32>

The rich perfumes ascend in waving spires,
And altars blaze with consecrated fires;
The fair assembly moves with graceful air,
And leaves of laurel bind the flowing hair.
Niobe comes with all her royal race,
With charms unnumber'd, and superior grace:

Her Phrygian garments of delightful hue,
Inwove with gold, refulgent to the view,
Beyond description beautiful she moves
Like heav'nly Venus, 'midst her smiles and loves:
She views around the supplicating train,
And shakes her graceful head with stern disdain,

Proudly she turns around her lofty eyes,
And thus reviles celestial deities:
"What madness drives the Theban ladies fair
To give their incense to surrounding air?
"Say why this new sprung deity preferr'd?
Why vainly fancy your petitions heard?

Or say why Caeus offspring is obey'd,
While to my goddesship no tribute's paid?
For me no altars blaze with living fires,
No bullock bleeds, no frankincense transpires,
"Tho' Cadmus' palace, not unknown to fame,
And Phrygian nations all revere my name.

Where'er I turn my eyes vast wealth I find,
Lo! here an empress with a goddess join'd.
What, shall a Titaness be deify'd,
To whom the spacious earth a couch deny'd!
"Nor heav'n, nor earth, nor sea receiv'd your queen,
Till pitying Delos took the wand'rer in.

<33>

Round me what a large progeny is spread!
No frowns of fortune has my soul to dread.
What if indignant she decrease my train
More than Latona's number will remain;
"Then hence, ye Theban dames, hence haste away,
Nor longer off'rings to Latona pay;

Regard the orders of Amphion's spouse,
And take the leaves of laurel from your brows."
Niobe spoke. The Theban maids obey'd,
Their brows unbound, and left the rites unpaid.

<34>

The angry goddess heard, then silence broke
On Cynthus' summit, and indignant spoke;
"Phoebus! behold, thy mother in disgrace,
Who to no goddess yields the prior place
Except to Juno's self, who reigns above,
The spouse and sister of the thund'ring Jove.

"Niobe, sprung from Tantalus, inspires
Each Theban bosom with rebellious fires;
No reason her imperious temper quells,
But all her father in her tongue rebels;
Wrap her own sons for her blaspheming breath,
Apollo! wrap them in the shades of death."

Latona ceas'd, and ardent thus replies
The God, whose glory decks th' expanded skies.
"Cease thy complaints, mine be the task assign'd
To punish pride, and scourge the rebel mind."
This Phoebe join'd. — They wing their instant flight;
Thebes trembled as th' immortal pow'rs alight.

<35>

With clouds incompass'd glorious Phoebus stands;
The feather'd vengeance quiv'ring in his hands.
Near Cadmus' walls a plain extended lay,
Where Thebes' young princes pass'd in sport the day:
There the bold coursers bounded o'er the plains,
While their great masters held the golden reins.

Ismenus first the racing pastime led,
And rul'd the fury of his flying steed.
"Ah me," he sudden cries, with shrieking breath,
While in his breast he feels the shaft of death;
He drops the bridle on his courser's mane,
Before his eyes in shadows swims the plain,

He, the first-born of great Amphion's bed,
Was struck the first, first mingled with the dead.
Then didst thou, Sipylus, the language hear
Of fate portentous whistling in the air:
As when th' impending storm the sailor sees
He spreads his canvas to the fav'ring breeze,

So to thine horse thou gav'st the golden reins,
Gav'st him to rush impetuous o'er the plains:
But ah! a fatal shaft from Phoebus' hand
Smites thro' thy neck, and sinks thee on the sand.
Two other brothers were at wrestling found,
And in their pastime claspt each other round:

A shaft that instant from Apollo's hand
Transfixt them both, and stretcht them on the sand:
Together they their cruel fate bemoan'd,
Together languish'd, and together groan'd:
Together too th' unbodied spirits fled,
And sought the gloomy mansions of the dead.

<37>

Alphenor saw, and trembling at the view,
Beat his torn breast, that chang'd its snowy hue.
He flies to raise them in a kind embrace;
A brother's fondness triumphs in his face:
Alphenor fails in this fraternal deed,
A dart dispatch'd him (so the fates decreed:)

Soon as the arrow left the deadly wound,
His issuing entrails smoak'd upon the ground.
What woes on blooming Damasichon wait!
His sighs portend his near impending fate.
Just where the well-made leg begins to be,
And the soft sinews form the supple knee,

The youth sore wounded by the Delian god
Attempts t' extract the crime-avenging rod,
But, whilst he strives the will of fate t' avert,
Divine Apollo sends a second dart;
Swift thro' his throat the feather'd mischief flies,
Bereft of sense, he drops his head, and dies.

Young Ilioneus, the last, directs his pray'r,
And cries, "My life, ye gods celestial! spare."
Apollo heard, and pity touch'd his heart,
But ah! too late, for he had sent the dart:
Thou too, O Ilioneus, art doom'd to fall,
The fates refuse that arrow to recall.

<38>

On the swift wings of ever flying Fame
To Cadmus' palace soon the tidings came:
Niobe heard, and with indignant eyes
She thus express'd her anger and surprise:
"Why is such privilege to them allow'd?
Why thus insulted by the Delian god?

"Dwells there such mischief in the pow'rs above?
Why sleeps the vengeance of immortal Jove?"
For now Amphion too, with grief oppress'd,
Had plung'd the deadly dagger in his breast.
Niobe now, less haughty than before,
With lofty head directs her steps no more

She, who late told her pedigree divine,
And drove the Thebans from Latona's shrine,
How strangely chang'd! — yet beautiful in woe,
She weeps, nor weeps unpity'd by the foe.
On each pale corse[9] the wretched mother spread
Lay overwhelm'd with grief, and kiss'd her dead,

Then rais'd her arms, and thus, in accents slow,
"Be sated cruel Goddess! with my woe;
If I've offended, let these streaming eyes,
And let this sev'nfold funeral suffice:
Ah! take this wretched life you deign'd to save,
With them I too am carried to the grave.

"Rejoice triumphant, my victorious foe,
But show the cause from whence your triumphs flow?
Tho' I unhappy mourn these children slain,
Yet greater numbers to my lot remain."
She ceas'd, the bow string twang'd with awful sound,
Which struck with terror all th' assembly round,

---

9 *Corse.* Corpse.

<39>

Except the queen, who stood unmov'd alone,
By her distresses more presumptuous grown.
Near the pale corses stood their sisters fair
In sable vestures and dishevell'd hair;
One, while she draws the fatal shaft away,
Faints, falls, and sickens at the light of day.

To soothe her mother, lo! another flies,
And blames the fury of inclement skies,
And, while her words a filial pity show,
Struck dumb — indignant seeks the shades below.
Now from the fatal place another flies,

Falls in her flight, and languishes, and dies.
Another on her sister drops in death;
A fifth in trembling terrors yields her breath;
While the sixth seeks some gloomy cave in vain,
Struck with the rest, and mingled with the slain.

One only daughter lives, and she the least;
The queen close clasp'd the daughter to her breast:
"Ye heav'nly pow'rs, ah spare me one," she cry'd,
"Ah! spare me one," the vocal hills reply'd:
In vain she begs, the Fates her suit deny,
In her embrace she sees her daughter die.

[The following lines were added by another hand:]

The queen of all her family bereft,
Without or husband, son, or daughter left,
Grew stupid at the shock. The passing air
Made no impression on her stiff'ning hair.
The blood forsook her face: amidst the flood
Pour'd from her cheeks, quite fix'd her eye-balls stood.
Her tongue, her palate both obdurate grew,
Her curdled veins no longer motion knew;
The use of neck, and arms, and feet was gone,
And ev'n her bowels hard'ned into stone:
A marble statue now the queen appears,
But from the marble steal the silent tears.

<41>

THE STORY OF NIOBE

by Samuel Croxall

*From Book VI of Garth's English Translation
of Ovid's* Metamorphoses (1717)

1

Swift thro' the Phrygian towns the rumour flies,
And the strange news each female tongue employs:
Niobe, who before she married knew
The famous nymph, now found the story true;
Yet, unreclaim'd by poor Arachne's fate,
Vainly above the Gods assum'd a state.
Her husband's fame, their family's descent,
Their pow'r, and rich dominion's wide extent,
Might well have justify'd a decent pride;
But not on these alone the dame rely'd.
Her lovely progeny, that far excell'd,
The mother's heart with vain ambition swell'd:
The happiest mother not unjustly syl'd,
Had no conceited thoughts her tow'ring fancy fill'd.
For once a prophetess with zeal inspir'd,
Their slow neglect to warm devotion fir'd;
Thro' ev'ry street of Thebes who ran possess'd,
And thus in accents wild her charge express'd:
"Haste, haste, ye Theban matrons, and adore,
With hallow'd rites, Latona's mighty pow'r;
And, to the heav'nly twins that from her spring,
With laurel crown'd, your smoaking incense bring."
Strait the great summons ev'ry dame obey'd,
And due submission to the Goddess paid:
Graceful, with laurel chaplets dress'd, they came,
And offer'd incense in the sacred flame.
Mean-while, surrounded with a courtly guard,
The royal Niobe in state appear'd;
Attir'd in robes embroider'd o'er with gold,
And mad with rage, yet lovely to behold:

<43>

High, on the top of Cynthus' shady mount,
With grief the Goddess saw the base affront;
And, the abuse revolving in her breast,
The mother her twin-offspring thus addrest.
"Lo I, my children, who with comfort knew
Your God-like birth, and thence my glory drew;
And thence have claim'd precedency of place
From all but Juno of the heav'nly race,
Must now despair, and languish in disgrace.
My godhead question'd, and all rites divine,
Unless you succour, banish'd from my shrine.
Nay more, the imp of Tantalus has flung
Reflections with her vile paternal tongue;
Has dar'd prefer her mortal breed to mine,
And call'd me childless; which, just fate, may she repine!"
When to urge more the Goddess was prepar'd,
Phoebus in haste replies, "Too much we've heard,
And ev'ry moment's lost, while vengeance is defer'd."
Diana spoke the same. Then both enshroud
Their heav'nly bodies in a sable cloud;
And to the Theban tow'rs descending light,
Thro' the soft yielding air direct their flight.

<46>

Without the wall there lies a champian ground
With even surface, far extending round,
Beaten and level'd, while it daily feels
The trampling horse, and chariot's grinding wheels.
Part of proud Niobe's young rival breed,
Practising there to ride the manag'd steed,
Their bridles boss'd with gold, were mounted high
On stately furniture of Tyrian dye.
Of these, Ismenos, who by birth had been
The first fair issue of the fruitful queen,
Just as he drew the rein to guide his horse,
Around the compass of the circling course,
Sigh'd deeply, and the pangs of smart express'd,
While the shaft stuck, engor'd within his breast:
And, the reins dropping from his dying hand,
He sunk quite down, and tumbled on the sand.
Sipylus next the rattling quiver heard,
And with full speed for his escape prepar'd;
As when the pilot from the black'ning skies
A gath'ring storm of wintry rain descries,
His sails unfurl'd, and crowded all with wind,
He strives to leave the threat'ning cloud behind:
So fled the youth; but an unerring dart
O'ertook him, quick discharg'd, and sped with art;
Fix'd in his neck behind, it trembling stood,
And at his throat display'd the point besmear'd with blood
Prone, as his posture was, he tumbled o'er,
And bath'd his courser's mane with steaming gore.
Next at young Phaedimus they took their aim,
And Tantalus who bore his grandsire's name:
These, when their other exercise was done,
To try the wrestler's oily sport begun;
And, straining ev'ry nerve, their skill express'd
In closest grapple, joining breast to breast:
When from the bending bow an arrow sent,
Joyn'd as they were, thro' both their bodies went:
Both groan'd, and writhing both their limbs with pain,
They fell together bleeding on the plain;

<47>

Then both their languid eye-balls faintly roll,
And thus together breathe away their soul.
With grief Alphenor saw their doleful plight,
And smote his breast, and sicken'd at the sight;
Then to their succor ran with eager haste,
And, fondly griev'd, their stiff'ning limbs embrac'd;
But in the action falls: a thrilling dart,
By Phoebus guided, pierc'd him to the heart.
This, as they drew it forth, his midriff tore,
Its barbed point the fleshy fragments bore,
And let the soul gush out in streams of purple gore.
But Damasichthon, by a double wound,
Beardless, and young, lay gasping on the ground.
Fix'd in his sinewy ham, the steely point
Stuck thro' his knee, and pierc'd the nervous joint:
And, as he stoop'd to tug the painful dart,
Another struck him in a vital part;
Shot thro' his wezon,[10] by the wing it hung.
The life-blood forc'd it out, and darting upward sprung,
Ilioneus, the last, with terror stands,
Lifting in pray'r his unavailing hands;
And, ignorant from whom his griefs arise,
"Spare me, o all ye heav'nly Pow'rs," he cries:
Phoebus was touch'd too late, the sounding bow
Had sent the shaft, and struck the fatal blow;
Which yet but gently gor'd his tender side,
So by a slight and easy wound he dy'd.

Facing Page: Anicet Charles Gabriel Lemonnier (1743-1824).
Niobe and Her Children Killed by Apollo and Artemis. (1772).

---

[10] *Wezon.* Weasand, or windpipe.

<49>

family, she received nothing from the estate of her former mistress. The poet's British connections were useless after the war, and Bostonians, who had failed to support the poet's first attempt at subscriptions for a book publication, failed twice more in her lifetime to subscribe to another offered book (1779 and again in 1784). In 1786, two years after her death, the first American edition of her work was brought out in Philadelphia.

NIOBE'S TEARS: WHEATLEY REWRITES OVID

Wheatley's longest extant poem, "Niobe in Distress for Her Children Slain by Apollo," is an adaptation of an episode in Book VI of Ovid's *Metamorphoses*.

Wheatley studied Latin, presumably with the Boston minister and poet Mather Byles, and had access, from his extensive library, to the classical translations of Dryden, Pope and others. Why, of all the stories available from Ovid and other sources, did Wheatley choose this particular tale of unremitting cruelty and slaughter, a tale without a tinge of meaning to Christian readers? (It is telling that both Dryden and Pope side-stepped the Niobe episode, leaving it to a younger poet, Samuel Croxall (d. 1752) when it came time to publish a complete *Metamorphoses* in English in 1717, under the editorship of Sir Samuel Garth.) It is doubtful that Wheatley saw the earlier, and rather rare translation by Arthur Golding from 1567, and its more remote English would not have served her well.

Wheatley's choice of this particular Ovid story is partly explained in her own words: the visual impetus she received on seeing the painting of Niobe by British artist Richard Wilson (1713?-1782). Wilson's *The Destruction of the Children of Niobe* was a landmark work, the first to combine English landscape painting with mythological figures. Did she see this renowned canvas during her visit to London, since she toured the British Museum? Probably not, as two Wilson Niobe paintings were privately owned, and the poem was already on press in her *Poems on Various Subjects* when she arrived in London in 1773. A print of a *second* Wilson Niobe canvas, engraved by William Wollett in 1761, had wide circulation on both sides of the Atlantic, and it is almost certain that this, and/or some as-yet-unidentified print of the *first* painting, was Wheatley's inspiration. As we will see, her poem is a combination of Ovidian translation and *ekphrasis* (poetic description of a work of visual art).

Wilson's dramatic canvas compresses the cruel action of the myth into a single scene. In the poem, the arrows of Apollo and Artemis kill Niobe's fourteen sons and daughters; in the painting, the figure of Artemis rises behind Apollo as he shoots from atop a rock through the branches of a menacing tree. Niobe tries to shield her youngest daughter, as her other offspring, in the various attitudes described by Ovid, expire. Crashing

<56>

waves, high cliffs, a gloomy castle, thunder-blasted tree trunks, and ominous clouds fill out the landscape.

Why else did the poet choose this panorama of slaughter as her subject? Wheatley had been torn from her own African family by slave traders, and may have been separated yet again from near relatives at the auction block in America. Is not Niobe the iconic image of a mother watching powerless as her children are hunted down?

This equation of violent separation with death would be echoed by African-American women. A later slave writer, Harriet Jacobs, writes of the plight of the slave mother who saw all her children auctioned off: "I met that mother in the street, and her wild, haggard face lives to-day in my mind. She wrung her hands in anguish, and exclaimed, 'Gone! All gone! Why don't God kill me?'" (Jacobs 16).

The cruel Apollo/Phoebus and Artemis/Phoebe, classic hunter figures, stand in for slave hunters quite readily. Further, Apollo, Phoebe and their wrathful mother Latona are all Titans, not subject to the law of Zeus, and hence stand in for amoral, rogue nations engaged in the slave trade and answerable to no higher authority. Cruelty in this classic realm can make no appeal to Christian charity or mercy.

A yeoman poet might have simply translated Ovid line for line, or paraphrased Croxall's couplets from the Garth edition of Ovid. Wheatley does something very different. Structurally, she breaks her narrative away from Ovid's daisy-chained pattern in which each episode provides a "hook" into the next. *Her* Niobe is to be an "epyllion," a self-contained miniature epic.

She begins with an invocation to the Muse, a cautious one since the theme is "Apollo's wrath to man." She offers to present both "What Wilson painted, and what Ovid wrote" thus promising both paraphrase and ekphrasis. Wheatley next provides a genealogy of Queen Niobe, moving the Queen's own awkward genealogical utterances from later in the episode into third-person narration.

The plot of "Niobe" is simple, and brutal. Niobe, descended from Titans and Zeus, is married to King Amphion, himself a mortal and a child of Zeus. Blessed with seven sons and seven daughters, Niobe has everything a monarch could want, except divinity. Both Wheatley and Croxall follow Ovid's telling of a prophetess who arrives in Thebes, demanding that the women light incense and make offerings to Latona and her children, Apollo/Phoebus and Artemis/Phoebe/Diana. Niobe orders the ceremonies halted, boasting that she has fourteen children while Latona has only two.

Wheatley provides the same information as Croxall, much the same in detail, but she re-arranges everything to create her own heroic couplets. What she moves to her genealogical prologue, she takes away from the mouth of Niobe. In doing so, she removes an exceedingly feeble couplet from Croxall: "Seven are my daughters, of a form divine,/ With seven fair

<57>

sons, an indefective line" (the "indefective" sounding exceedingly awkward), while Wheatley's omniscient narrator offers "Seven sprightly sons the royal bed adorn,/ Seven daughters beauteous as the op'ning morn" (23-24), with its string of sibilants and its curious eleven-syllable lines breaking the iambic pentameter mold of the poem for effect.

When Latona summons Apollo and Artemis to take action, Croxall says rather awkwardly: "The mother her twin-offspring thus addrest"; Wheatley simply has Latona call out "Phoebus! Behold thy mother in disgrace" (91).

Here Wheatley inserts two lines inspired by the Wilson painting: "With clouds encompass'd glorious Phoebus stands;/ The feather'd vengeance quiv'ring in his hands" (107-108), two good lines, even throwing in a nice word play of arrows as "feather'd vengeance" and the verb "quivering" playing against the noun "quiver," the case that contains an archer's arrows. It was noted as far back as 1866 that these fine lines are not in Ovid, and Shields documented the engraving of Wilson's painting as the likely visual inspiration (Shields, Wheatley 292).

The lines not only delight in their word-play, but provide scenic or stage-like quality to the narration, missing from Ovid at this moment. Wheatley has read her Homer, and she is not outdone by Croxall in describing death. The arrow-slaying of the oldest son Ismenos, in Croxall's lines, is "[He] Sigh'd deeply, and the pangs of smart express'd,/ While the shaft stuck, engor'd within his breast." Croxall's first line sounds more like a bee sting than a fatal blow, while Wheatley writes: "'Ah, me', he sudden cries, with shrieking breath,/ While in his breast he feels the shaft of death." Wheatley adds a Homeric line of her own, "Before his eyes in shadow swim the plain."

Death for death, Croxall and Wheatley are well matched. To this reader, Wheatley is often the better. In the death of two brothers, impaled with a single arrow as they wrestle, Wheatley, following Ovid's Latin, breaks the usual English avoidance of anaphora and phrase repetition in this kind of writing (you will almost never find it in epics in English) and gives three lines with a refrain word, "together":

Together they their cruel fate bemoan'd,
Together languish'd, and together groan'd
Together too th'unbodied spirits fled,
And sought the gloomy mansions of the dead (133-136).

When the last son, Ilioneus, prays, an instant too late, to be spared by the gods. Apollo wishes to call back his arrow, but cannot. As if to suspend the reader in time, in the instant before the arrow strikes and kills, Wheatley jumps to future tense. In what is either very bad writing, or very good

<58>

writing indeed, the stanza actually stutters in time, shifting tenses thus: present, past, past perfect, future, and present, with good effect:

> Young Ilioneus, the last, directs his pray'r,
> And cries, "My life, ye gods celestial! spare."
> Apollo heard, and pity touch'd his heart,
> But ah! too late, for he had sent the dart:
> Thou, too, Ilioneus, art doom'd to fall,
> The fates refuse that arrow to recall. (155-160)

Niobe's rage over her sons' deaths leads to another boast, and then, in turn, to the killing of her seven daughters as they bend over their slain or dying brothers. Wheatley introduces into Niobe's cry of outrage a reference to Zeus/Jove not found in Croxall: "Why sleeps the vengeance of immortal Jove?" (168). She is asking why the father of gods permits this, and here she is all mothers, pagan, Christian, slave. Wheatley's introduction of this "Why" is poignant.

Croxall scores a sublime point with the line, "Feast your black malice at a price thus dear," and Wheatley does not even try approach this. As Niobe shelters the last daughter with her robes and body, Croxall has the queen plead, "Only for this, the youngest, I implore,/ Grant me this one request, I ask no more", a very courteous request.

Wheatley's Niobe goes closer to the heart: "'Ye heav'nly powers, ah spare me one,' she cried,/ 'Ah spare me one,' the vocal hills reply'd" (209-210). Wheatley adds the Greek "echo" here, although it is not in Ovid or Croxall, and critics who have commented on this innovation seem to have missed one likely reason for it: Wilson's painting frames the murders with a background of hills and stark cliffs, a sounding board for echoes.

Croxall carries the story through Niobe's mourning, petrifaction, and relocation as a perennially weeping rock. Following Ovid, Croxall also adds the "hook" to the succeeding episode. Wheatley offers no denouement, no moral. She leaves the bereft Niobe at the death of her last daughter: "In her embrace she sees her daughter die." (Additional lines closing the poem were added, but they were not of Wheatley's composition.) The poet's "first thought-best thought" leaves us with stark horror, the frozen moment depicted in Wilson's painting, the mother bereft of children in Thebes, in Africa, at the auction block.

Just as Wilson's choice of tableau as a painter is to show Apollo in action, Niobe's children in their death throes, and Niobe in supplication, Wheatley's choice as a poet is to leave the reader in the moment after all that can happen to Niobe as mother has happened, an instant of stupefied horror as the last child dies in her protective embrace.

<59>

In a 1980 article on Wheatley's use of classicism, neither John C. Shields nor the earlier critics he cites seem to have connected all the novelties in "Niobe" with the Wilson painting. Shields does agree that Wheatley's ending is intentional and effective, and is ready to grant her the laurel she was striving for: "Epiclike poems which exhibit both an intimate familiarity with epic properties and, more importantly, a capacity to re-arrange those properties in such a way that she constructs original works" (111).

WHEATLEY AND THE CLASSICAL DISCOURSE

Marsha Watson, another scholar finding merit in Wheatley's classical poetry, concurs that "[T]o read poetry through a post-Romantic lens is fundamentally a viewpoint that finds neoclassical phrasing baroque, insincere, and repetitive (105) ... [I]n refusing to acknowledge the multiple layers of Wheatley's neoclassical poetic language, critics have refused to acknowledge her intertextuality, instead deeming her interaction with Anglo-European writers 'imitative'" (110). If one denies that a Boston slave could absorb and create anew from Homer or Ovid authentically, how can one then claim that an Englishman of the 18th century had such an ability, or an Italian of the Renaissance, or a monk of the Middle Ages? Such a claim cancels the whole idea of the art's universality.

Revising a long-held feeling that Wheatley was writing "white" religious poetry and not aware of or willing to serve the cause of her own people, some scholars now see her as a "subtle warrior" (O'Neale 1986), well versed in abolitionist issues and personally familiar with many of the clergymen fighting for abolition (Levemier 1991). I would contend that "Niobe," read symbolically as the plea of the bereaved African mother for justice, is Wheatley's way of using classical means to convey the enslaved peoples' plea to a different audience: readers with an Enlightenment outlook outside the fold of theology.

It is interesting to note that, after the Revolution, Wheatley attempted to write poems that syncretized classical allusions with contemporary politics. Britannia would give way to Columbia, as both the American and French Revolutions sought secular myth-making. Wheatley was willing to move with the times, and to inhabit territory beyond that of her Christian occasional poems.

Wheatley's other poems in a neoclassical vein also await an extended examination. One that I find striking may be the first "coded" allusion to Greek homoeroticism in American poetry. Wheatley's poems-in-dialogue with two British sailors contain a striking allusion to *The Iliad*. Wheatley suggests that the sailor Rochfort is so handsome that if he had gone to Troy

<60>

with the Greeks, that Paris would have given up Helen in order to be his friend. The three poems' playful banter and Wheatley's further reference to the two sailors' friendship with one another, make it one of those classical pieces of a special sort: Platonic and innocent to the uninitiated, but full of import for Boston's classically-inclined "bachelor society."

TO A GENTLEMAN OF THE NAVY (1774)

Paris, for Helen's resistless charms
Made Ilion bleed and set the world in arms.
Had you appear'd on the Achaian shore
Troy now had stood, and Helen charm'd no more.
The Phrygian hero had resign'd the dame
For purer joys in friendship's sacred flame,
The noblest gift, and of immortal kind,
That brightens, dignifies, the manly mind.

Thanks to the work of William Bennemann and B.R. Burg, we now know that colonial Philadelphia and Boston, at least, harbored small gay communities, and that the world of sailors was a complex and sexually unorthodox one. The History Project in Boston, in its documentary work, has also uncovered traces of that city's suppressed gay colonial history, published as *Improper Bostonians*. Reading below the surface of Wheatley's "sailor" poems puts her in dialogue with these freer spirits, a Boston "underground" that would have appreciated and encouraged her classical mode.

I also find it intriguing that Wheatley wrote two poems attacking atheists and deists, but then omitted them from her published book, and from her two failed prospectuses for a second volume. This meant, first, that she was engaged in lively debate with persons holding those opinions, and that she finally thought better of her disdain for them. Her own life experience, before and after being freed, taught her that Power is not merciful, and that Piety is not kind.

Religion, it would now appear, did not "produce" Phillis Wheatley. Her Christian sponsors would lock her in a room and order her to produce a poem on demand, in order to demonstrate to others how Christianity had "saved" her from her "savage" origins. Wheatley cannot be confined as a Christianized slave, an abolitionist, or even as an African American woman writer, even though those who first published her capitalized on these identities. With "Niobe," she lays claim to an identity that has been denied her: that of poet in the community of poets. Phillis Wheatley, your time has come.

<61>

The BLOODY MASSACRE perpetrated in King—t—Street BOSTON on March 5th 1770 by a party of the 29th REGt.

Engrav'd Printed & Sold by PAUL REVERE BOSTON

BUTCHERS HALL

Unhappy Boston! see thy Sons deplore,
Thy hallow'd Walks besmear'd with guiltless Gore.
While faithless P——n and his savage Bands,
With murd'rous Rancour stretch their bloody Hands;
Like fierce Barbarians grinning o'er their Prey,
Approve the Carnage, and enjoy the Day.

If scalding drops from Rage from Anguish Wrung
If speechless Sorrows lab'ring for a Tongue,
Or if a weeping World can ought appease
The plaintive Ghosts of Victims such as these;
The Patriot's copious Tears for each are shed,
A glorious Tribute which embalms the Dead.

But know, Fate summons to that awful Goal,
Where Justice strips the Murd'rer of his Soul:
Should venal C——ts the scandal of the Land,
Snatch the relentless Villain from her Hand,
Keen Execrations on this Plate inscrib'd,
Shall reach a Judge who never can be brib'd.

Copy Right Secured.

The unhappy Sufferers were Messrs. SAML. GRAY, SAML. MAVERICK, JAMS. CALDWELL, CRISPUS ATTUCKS & PATK. CARR
Killed. Six wounded; two of them (CHRISTr. MONK & JOHN CLARK) Mortally

THE MYTH OF NIOBE
AND THE BOSTON MASSACRE

by Brett Rutherford

A S AN ADDENDUM to the preceding article on Phillis Wheatley's poem "Niobe in Distress for Her Children Slain by Apollo," I offer this brief article that brings into play Wheatley's poem, the Richard Wilson painting, and the famous engraving by Paul Revere of The Boston Massacre. There is both textual and visual evidence that Revere borrowed visual elements from an engraving of the Wilson painting, and intended the verse attached to the depiction of the massacre "Unhappy Boston," to allude to the myth of Niobe.

Paul Revere's 1770 engraving of The Boston Massacre is an icon of the American Revolution, and the best-known of the works in print from the Boston silversmith and engraver. Another engraver, Peter Pelham, did the original drawing and published it separately with some Biblical verses attached. Revere copied Pelham's drawing, and added the original verses that we know today. Revere's version prevailed, despite Pelham's original rights to the drawing. (Revere and Pelham later became business partners, so they apparently got over the dispute.)[11]

The synergy of verse to image is powerful, even though the drawing is crude and communicates in a short-hand almost like a modern comic book.

Among the crowd of people on the "victim" side of the engraving stands a woman wrapped in a shawl, her hands clasped in agony. She has her elbows spread out, and she shelters two children, whose heads peep out over her shoulder. A Niobe-like figure indeed. Jay Fliegelman spots this in his analysis the engraving:

> [What] the engraving depicts is less the "outrage" committed by British troops than the "outrage" felt by patriots in response to it. It depicts and gives voice to what the poem printed below it calls "speechless sorrow lab'ring for a tongue," the kind of sorrow expressed in the countenance of the shawled woman behind the action on the left, who is the inscribed surrogate for the viewer of the print. (76)

---

[11] While Pelham was producing 575 prints for sale, Revere rushed ahead with his own version. Revere's prints went on sale March 26, 1770, Pelham's on April 9. (Forbes 161).

<63>

The verses by Paul Revere under the drawing are all about weeping and tears, inviting us to look for a personification in the drawing. Although "Boston" is personified in this female witness, Niobe is invoked by the "tears" reference, since the petrified Niobe weeps eternally. The anonymous verses, attributed to Revere himself (Goss 71), read in part:

Unhappy Boston! see thy Sons deplore,
Thy hallow'd Walks besmear'd with guiltless Gore.
While faithless P[resto]n and his savage Bands,
With murd'rous Rancour stretch their bloody hands;
Like fierce Barbarians grinning o'er their Prey,
Approve the Carnage and enjoy the Day.

If scalding drops from Rage from Anguish Wrung
If speechless Sorrows lab'ring for a Tongue,
Or if a weeping World can ought appease
The plaintive Ghosts of Victims such as these;
The Patriot's copious tears for each are shed,
A glorious Tribute which embalms the Dead

Turning next to Wilson's Niobe, it can be seen that the two corpses on the lower left of the Revere engraving are the same as corresponding figures in the Wilson canvas. Pelham, then, used Wilson's *Niobe* as a model for the drawing on which the engravings were made.

As to why an artist/engraver would crib images from another artist, it should be remembered that Pelham and Revere were not painters. The creation of a crowd scene in three-dimensional perspective is daunting even for a trained artist, often requiring posed sketches or "cartoons." It is understandable that, especially in the pinch of time, the Boston printmakers would turn to fine art on hand to find subjects suitably posed. Historian Esther Forbes concurs, writing, "No engraver had many scruples about using other men's works or copying the designs of artists. Paul Revere had none at all . . . Paul Revere could not draw, and he knew it (110-111)."

The Pelham and Revere engravings show a puff of smoke from a chimney. It has the same contour as the cloud from which Apollo and Artemis unleash their arrows in Wilson's painting.

The other "cloud" in the print is the roiling mass of smoke from the firing guns of the British soldiers. Like the mysterious hovering cloud from which Apollo and Artemis do their slaying, the smoke shown here is a comic-book fantasy. Only a single volley was fired, so what is shown is impossible: in the same instant, the order to fire is being given; the shots

Facing page: Richard Wilson's *The Destruction of the Children of Niobe*.
(Only available photo).

<64>

are in the air; the victims have already fallen; and the smoke that *follows* the shots is a dense cloud enveloping the troops. This visual short-hand brings us back to the victims, telling us in an accordioned way, the actions they have just witnessed.

Pelham and Revere also outline a waxing crescent moon, which turns out to be incorrect for the date. The night of the massacre was a half-moon (Korsmeyer 260). The waxing crescent moon is associated with Artemis/Diana and is known as "Diana's Bow."

Did Wheatley have anything to do with the classical allusion in Revere's print? There is no evidence for this, but she was well-known in Boston and many had seen her poems, even though "Niobe" would have existed then only in manuscript. It might have been common knowledge that Phillis, the then 17-year-old slave poet, had written a mini-epic on Ovid, and that Niobe was the subject. What is more in evidence is that the story of Niobe was part of the common cultural inheritance. Those who read Latin, knew it from the original, and it had been conspicuously available in English since the 1717 London edition edited by Garth. As a separate fable, it may have been mentioned in sermons as a pagan example of "Pride goeth before a fall." (One guidebook long available to ministers to provide comfortable morals from the *Metamorphoses* was titled *Ovid Moralisé*.)

We do not know the date of composition for Wheatley's "Niobe" poem, but there is a curious reference to political rebellion that suggests it was revised or completed *after* the Boston Massacre, from several phrases that do not come from Ovid or from Croxall's English version (italics mine):

Niobe sprung from Tantalus *inspires*
Each Theban bosom with rebellious fires;
No reason her imperious temper quells,
But all her father in her tongue *rebels* ...

To punish pride, and *scourge the rebel mind*. (l. 95-104)

By adding rebellion to hubris, Wheatley indicts Niobe as a political figure personifying Thebes, thus joining the two massacres as political acts. Instead of victims, "rebels."

Wheatley's poem to the Earl of Dartmouth, in her published book, speaks up for the colonies against oppression, and then speaks (ironically it would seem) in her own voice as a slave.

The slave-poet's own poem on The Boston Massacre, titled "The Affray at King Street," was not included in her printed volume, and never saw print; the manuscript has never been found. But the following poem was

<66>

published anonymously on March 12th, a week after the massacre, in the *Boston Evening Post.* It is now considered to be Wheatley's "lost" poem.

THE AFFRAY IN KING STREET
With Fire enrap't, surcharg'd with sudden Death,
Lo! the pois'd Tube convolves its fatal breath!
The flying ball with heaven-directed Force,
Rids the Spirit of the fallen corse.
Well sated Shades! Let no unwomanly Tear
From Pity's Eye, disdain in your honour'd Bier;
Lost to the View, surviving friends may mourn,
Yet on thy Pile shall Flames celestial burn;
Long as in *Freedom's* Cause the Wise contend,
Dear to your unity shall Fame extend;
While to the World, the letter'd Stone shall tell
How *Caldwell, Attucks, Gray,* and *Mav'rick* fell.

In sum, what we may safely say is that Wheatley was "in the know." The Wheatley family lived on King Street. The young poet may have slipped the poem of protest into the newspaper under the nose of her Tory "family" within days of the massacre. Did Revere know about her "Niobe?"

RICHARD WILSON AND THE MULTIPLE NIOBES

Richard Wilson's *The Destruction of the Children of Niobe* (1760), is shown on the preceding page in an old black-and-white photo taken before 1943. The painting, modest as it now seems, created a sensation as it was the first time an English painter had added classical human figures to a traditional landscape painting. Unlike the classic sculptural presentations from antiquity that centered on the suffering of the human form in isolation, and unlike the Romantic paintings that would follow that filled the canvas to the edges with toppled victims and horses, so crowded that hardly a branch intruded, Wilson's canvas has gods and humans as tiny figures in a *sturm-und-drang* landscape with cliffs, waterfalls, lightning, menacing clouds, fierce winds, and a storm-blasted tree. Nature is the stage: the gods and humans are the actors within it.

On the succeeding pages: Another *Niobe* canvas by Richard Wilson, now at Yale, and a detail of the backwards-drawn engraving from it by Wollett.

<67>

The painting was in Britain and its appearance was known only from etchings and engravings. Such prints crossed the Atlantic and were avidly collected. The best were faithful reproductions in the engraver's line and tone, and artists were paid to add watercolor tints to the prints.

The engraving that Wheatley saw has not been identified, but we know from a later engraving that this painting was in the collection of Sir George Beaumont, and the 1792 engraving by Samuel Smith and William Sharp is captioned, "From the FIRST PICTURE on that subject painted by Richard Wilson." By 1832, the painting was in the National Gallery and an authorized engraving by S. Lacey was issued; again, this print agrees in every detail with the photo shown.

A few words are in order about the other *Niobes*, since a casual search for Wilson's paintings can lead one astray. Like many painters with a success on his hands, Wilson made more "Niobe" paintings, at least four of them. In them he placed Apollo and Diana, and similar Niobid victims, in different landscapes. One canvas is at the Yale Center for British Art. The very famous engraving of Wilson's Niobe by William Wollett, produced in 1761, was indeed known in Boston as it was widely advertised as one of the best (and costliest) art prints of its time. Curiously, Wollett inverts the entire Wilson canvas. It is not a mirror-reverse as an engraving or woodblock master would appear to the eye. In fact, Wollett has redrawn the whole painting, with great elegance, with special attention to a sprawling bushy tree that dominates the landscape. But all the human figures are re-posed in this reversed landscape. Wollett pulls it off, except for one inevitable flaw: his Apollo, now at the far-right, has now become a left-handed archer! A detail of the painting at Yale is included here, and, after that, a detail from the Wollett engraving.

It is indeed possible that Wheatley saw the Wollett engraving of this alternate *Niobe*, but I believe she, and Revere, also had access to an engraving of the original *Niobe* painting. I hope this will come to light.

A third Wilson *Niobe* canvas, now dated 1768, is in the National Library of Wales. Shown here at left, it contains no Apollo or Diana, and only three victim figures. The painting includes a lightning-strike, crashing waves, and a huge, burning funeral pyre.

For the purpose of studying the "first" Niobe painting, we have only the black-and-white photo of the canvas, and the later engravings to the extent that they reproduce its details faithfully. This is all we have, for the Wilson painting that concerns us most was destroyed as surely as Niobe's children, during the Nazi bombing of London, sometime in 1943.

Facing page: Another Wilson *Niobe* painting, now at the National Library of Wales.

<71>

The shawled female spectator in Pelham and Revere's print,
with children's faces behind her.

Artemis/Diana with moon in "Diana's Bow"
form, from a French Niobe painting.

<72>

Note the shape of the cloud from which Apollo and Artemis shoot their arrows, in Wilson's painting.

The same shape is used for the puff of chimney smoke in Pelham and Revere's prints, under the "Diana's Bow," which was not the correct moon phase for the night of the massacre.

<73>

Pelham and Revere place two corpses in similar poses to those in the Wilson Niobe painting. The body on the right is turned over, one arm extended, so that his face shows with a bleeding wound. The figure on the left has the same pose as the corresponding victim in Wilson, right knee raised. Pelham copies the extended fold of cloth on the ground from the Wilson canvas.

<74>

BIBLIOGRAPHY

Adams, Nehemiah. *A South-Side View of Slavery; or Three Months at the South in 1854*. 1855. Boston: T. R. Martin.

Andrews, William Loring. *Paul Revere and His Engraving*. New York: Scribner's, 1901.

Banier, Abbé. *Banier's Ovid Commentary Englished*. 1732. Accessed from etext.lib.virginia.edu/latin/ovid/banier.html.

Benemann, William. *Male-Male Intimacy in Early America: Beyond Romantic Friendships*. 2006. New York: Harrington Park Press.

Bly, Antonio T. "Wheatley's on the Affray in King Street." *The Explicator,* Vol. 56 No 4, 1998.

Brigham, Clarence. *Paul Revere's Engravings*. New York: Atheneum, 1969.

Bull, Malcolm. *The Mirror of the Gods*. Oxford: Oxford University Press, 2005. [Includes a detailed history of illustrated editions of *The Metamorphoses*.]

Burg, B.R. *Gay Warriors: A Documentary History from the Ancient World to the Present*. 2002. New York: New York University Press.

Byles, Mather. *Poems on Several Occasions*. Boston: n.p., 1744.

Carretta, Vincent. "Phillis Wheatley, the Mansfield Decision of 1772, and the Choice of Identity." *Early America Re-Explored: New Readings in Colonial, Early National, and Antebellum Culture*. Edited by Klaus H. Schmidt and Fritz Fleischmann. Early American Literature and Culture through the American Renaissance. New York: Peter Lang, 2000. 201-24.

Eaton, Arthur W. H. *The Famous Mather Byles: The Noted Boston Tory Preacher, Poet and Wit*. Boston: W. A. Butterfield, 1914.

Fliegelman, Jay. *Declaring Independence: Jefferson, Natural Language, and the Culture of Performance*. Stanford: Stanford U Press, 1993.

Forbes, Esther. *Paul Revere and the World He Lived In*. Boston: Houghton Mifflin, 1942.

Gates, Henry Louis, Jr. *The Trials of Phillis Wheatley: America's First Black Poet and Her Encounters with the Founding Fathers*. New York: Basic Civitas, 2003.

Godwin, Jocelyn. *The Pagan Dream of the Renaissance*. Grand Rapids, MI: Phanes Press, 2002.

Goss, Elbridge Henry. *The Life of Colonel Paul Revere*. Vol. 1. 2 vols. Boston: Joseph George Copple, 1891.

Grimsted, David. "Anglo-American Racism and Phillis Wheatley's 'Sable Veil,' 'Lengthened Chain' and 'Knitted Heart'." *Women in the American Revolution*. Edited by Ronald Hoffman and Peter J. Albert. Charlottesville, VA: U of VA Press, 1989.

<75>

Harding, Alan. *The Countess of Huntingdon's Connexion: A Sect in Action in Eighteenth-Century England.* 2003. Oxford: Oxford University Press.

Hayden, Lucy. "Classical Tidings from the Afric Muse: Phillis Wheatley's Use of Greek and Roman Mythology." *College Language Association Journal* 35.4 (1992): 432-47.

The History Project. *Improper Bostonians: Lesbian and Gay History from the Puritans to Playland.* 1998. Boston: Beacon Press.

Hughes, Louis. *Thirty Years A Slave: From Bondage to Freedom. The Institution of Slavery As Seen on the Plantation and in the Home of the Planter.* 1897. Milwaukee: South Side Printing Company.

Isani, Mukhtar Ali. "The British Reception of Wheatley's Poems on Various Subjects." *Journal of Negro History.* Vol. 66, No. 2, Summer 1981, pp. 144-149. [Reprints previously-unknown press reviews of Wheatley's poetry.]

Jacobs, Harriet A. *Incidents in the Life of a Slave Girl, Written by Herself 1861.* Cambridge: Harvard University Press, 2000.

Jefferson, Thomas. *Notes on the State of Virginia.* 1785. Edited by Frank Shuffleton. New York: Penguin, 1999.

Korsmeyer, Carolyn. "Pictorial Assertion." *Journal of Aesthetics and Art Criticism* 43.3 (1985): 257-65.

Langley, April. "Imagined Post-Coloniality and 'Natural' Coloniality: The Production of Space in Phillis Wheatley's 'Niobe in Distress for Her Children Slain by Apollo'." *Auto/Biography Studies* 16.1 (2001): 90-108.

Levernier, James A. "Phillis Wheatley and the New England Clergy." *Early American Literature* 26 (1991): 21-38.

O'Neale, Sondra. "A Slave's Subtle War: Phillis Wheatley's Use of Biblical Myth and Symbol." *Early American Literature* 21 (1986): 144-65.

Orchard, Stephen. "Evangelical Eschatology and the Missionary Awakening." *Journal of Religious History.* 22.2 June 1998. 132-151.

Ovid. *Metamorphoses.* Latin text with English translation by Frank Justis Miller. 1916. Cambridge, MA: Harvard University Press. Second edition, 1926.

Ovid. *Metamorphoses.* Edited by Samuel Garth. London: Jacob Tonson, 1717. [Includes the translation of "Niobe" by Samuel Croxall.]

Ovid. *The XV Bookes of P. Ovidius Naso, entytled Metamorphosis.* Translated by Arthur Golding. 1567. London: William Seres. [Reprinted in 1904 by De La More Press, London, edited by W. H. D. Rouse.]

Revere, Paul. *The Bloody Massacre Perpetrated in King Street, Boston, on March 5th 1770 by a Party of the 29th Regiment.* 1770. Paul Revere, Boston.

<76>

"Richard Wilson's Niobe." *The Burlington Magazine for Connoisseurs.* Vol. 85 No. 498, September 1944, pp. 210-213+215. jstor.com/stable/869043

Shields, John C. "Phillis Wheatley's Struggle for Freedom in Her Poetry and Prose." *The Collected Works of Phillis Wheatley.* New York: Oxford UP, 1988. 229-70.

---. "Phillis Wheatley's Use of Classicism." *American Literature* 52.1 (1980): 97-111.

Solkin, David H. *Richard Wilson: The Landscape of Reaction.* London: The Tate Gallery, 1982.

Watson, Marsha. "A Classic Case: Phillis Wheatley and Her Poetry." *Early American Literature* 31 (1996): 103-32.

Wheatley, Phillis. *The Collected Works of Phillis Wheatley.* Edited by John C. Shields. New York: Oxford University Press, 1988.

---. "On the Affray in King Street." Published anonymously in *The Boston Evening Post.* March 12, 1770.

<77>

ART CREDITS

◆————————◆

Not all illustrations in this book have captions, in order not to interfere with the flow of the poems. See below for specific page numbers.

Cover: Anicet Charles Gabriel Lemonnier (1743-1824). *Niobe and Her Children Killed by Apollo and Artemis.* (1772). Oil on paper. Musée des Beaux-Arts de Rouen. Image from Wikimedia Commons.

Frontispiece: Jacques Louis David (1748-1825). *Niobe and Her Daughter.* (1775-80). Black ink with gray wash on paper. National Gallery of Art. Creative Commons Public Domain.

Running heads over titles: Roman sarcophagus: *Apollo and Artemis killing the Fourteen children of Niobe* (front side). Artemis; five daughters with a nurse; younger son with a pedagogue; three other sons; Apollo. Top: dead Niobids. 160–170 CE. Found near the Via Appia in 1824. Glyphotek Museum, Munich. Photo by Bibi Saint-Pol, from Wikimedia Commons.

Page 8. Portrait of Phillis Wheatley, London, September 1, 1773. Engraving by Scipio Moorhead.

Page 12. *Wounded Niobid.* Parian marble, Greek artwork, c. 440 BCE. From the Horti Sallustiana in the area of Piazza Sallustio, Rome. Palazzo Massimo alle Terma, Rome. Photograph by Jastrow, 2006. From Wikimedia Commons.

Details on pp. 20, 28, 30. Abraham Bloemaert. *Apollo and Diana Punishing Niobe by Killing her Children.* 1591. Oil on canvas. Statens Museum for Kunst. From Wikimedia Commons.

Details on pp. 24, 26. Andrea Camassei (1602-1649). *The Massacre of the Niobids* (1638-1639). Oil on canvas. Galleria Nazionale d'Arte Antica, Rome. Public domain image from Wikimedia.

Details on pp. 36, 40. Jacques Louis David (1748-1825). *Apollo and Diana Attacking the Children of Niobe* (1772). Oil on canvas. Dallas Museum of Art. From Wikimedia Commons.

Detail on page 42. Pierre-Charles Jombert (1748-1825). *Niobe's Children Are Killed by Apollo and Diana* (1772).

Page 65. Richard Wilson. *The Destruction of the Children of Niobe.* Black-and-white photo only; original destroyed in World War II.

Page 68. Richard Wilson. *The Destruction of the Children of Niobe.* (1760?). Yale Center for British Art.

Page 69. William Wollet (Engraver). *Niobe, After the painting of Richard Wilson.* Wood engraving. Published by J. Boydell, Cheapside. London. 1761. (Based on the Niobe painting now at the Yale Center for British Art).

Page 70. Richard Wilson. *The Destruction of Niobe's Children* (1768). Oil con canvas. Llyfrgell Genedlaethol Cymru / The National Library of Wales.

<78>

ABOUT THIS BOOK

The body type for this book is set in Plantin, a typeface designed for Monotype in 1912, based on Renaissance Roman letter-forms found in the Plantin-Moretus Museum in Antwerp. The original designers were Frank Pierpont and Fritz Stelzer. The face moved into the digital era around 2001, and the Poet's Press has chosen it for its new standard typeface for print and ebooks, replacing Aldine.

Main titles and section titles are set in Geo Slab. Slab-serif typefaces began appearing early in the 19th century, and are still employed occasionally to evoke that era. Small titles are set in Century 725 Condensed, designed by Heinrich Hoffmeister, based on the classic Century family first created in 1894 by Linn Boyd Benton for American Type Founders, for use in *The Century Magazine*. It is used here in headlines, including small capitals, to suggest the days of metal typesetting.

<79>